DECORATIVE
STRAW CRAFT

To my husband Bill, and our children Peter, Julie and Tony, for their support and encouragement.

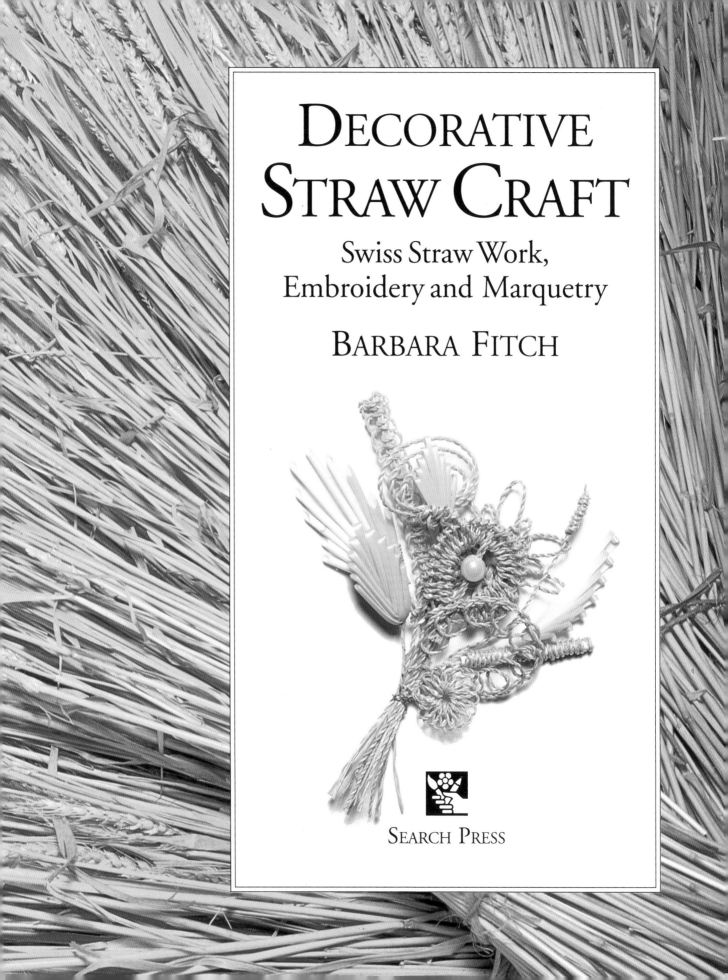

DECORATIVE STRAW CRAFT

Swiss Straw Work, Embroidery and Marquetry

BARBARA FITCH

SEARCH PRESS

First published in Great Britain 1998
Search Press Limited
Wellwood, North Farm Road,
Tunbridge Wells, Kent TN2 3DR

Text copyright © Barbara Fitch 1998

Photographs by Search Press Studios with the exception of those on pages 10, 14 and 15, which are reproduced by kind permission of J. Rudolf Isler, Wohlen, Switzerland. These photographs first appeared in *Strohzeiten*, published in German by AT Verlag. The original pieces are held in the Freiämter Straw Museum in Wohlen, Switzerland.

Photograph and design copyright © Search Press Ltd. 1998

ISBN 0 85532 824 X

Publisher's note
All the step-by-step photographs in this book feature the author Barbara Fitch. No models have been used.

Colour separation by P&W Graphics, Singapore
Printed in Spain by Elkar S. Coop, Bilbao 48012

I would like to give special thanks to J. Rudolf Isler, past-president of the Freiämter Straw Museum, Wohlen, Switzerland, for his friendship and generosity. Without his continued support and encouragement over the past ten years, this book would never have been written.

I would also like to thank all those who have shared their knowledge with me: Kim Miller, Thamesside Adult Education Institute; the late Alec Coker, Margaret Bradbury's Summer Schools at Much Cowarne, Herefordshire; Peter Shelley and Anne Dyer, Westhope College, Shropshire; Doris Johnson; the late Betty Blackwood; Dorothy Horsfall; the late Lena Croucher; Marian Nichols, Luton Museum; the curators of the Victoria and Albert Museum, the Bath Costume Museum and the Museum of London; the curator of Embroiderers' Guild museum collection at Hampton Court and, especially, the members of the London branch of the Embroiderers' Guild; Elizabeth Spinnler-Furrer, Brigette Koch, Mrs Späm, Ruth Rumo, Mrs Brugger, Mrs Rohr-Hunziker, Anny Hoppler – all from Switzerland; and finally, my editor, John Dalton, for his foresight and guidance.

Suppliers
If you have any difficulty in obtaining any of the materials and equipment mentioned in this book, please write to the publishers for a current list of stockists, which includes firms who operate a mail-order service:
Search Press Limited, Wellwood,
North Farm Road, Tunbridge Wells,
Kent TN2 3DR, England

Contents

Introduction

Two years after I started making corn dollies I was told about a museum in Switzerland that contained a collection of wonderful straw work. Together with fifteen other people, I visited the museum and immediately fell in love the range of beautiful exhibits. I was so fascinated by them that I began to research the techniques, and to make the designs myself. That was over ten years ago now, and my interest is as strong today as it was then; so much so, that I still regularly visit the museum, and correspond with the board of trustees.

The fundamental difference between corn dollies and the Swiss straw work described in this book, is that the latter is all constructed from narrow splints of straw – either as flat strips or as threads made by twisting splints together.

On the following pages, I show you how to make straw splints, how to twist them into thread and how to make a whole collection of delicate motifs that can be used to create wonderful designs.

I also show you how you can incorporate straw into embroideries and how to create straw veneers for marquetry.

Antique ornaments and an embroidered stole (circa 1835), all created using Swiss straw techniques.

History

The straw work described in this book has its roots in Switzerland and was developed over a period of nearly three hundred years. Sadly, the thriving cottage industry which designed all the wonderful straw braids and ornaments, and which made the town of Wohlen the centre of high fashion, has all but disappeared. The skills, that were once part of family life, are now known to only a few gifted people who are trying to keep the craft alive.

The earliest reference to fashionable straw work in Switzerland is to the *Schinhat* – a straw braid hat. This was stitched with a *rustic* braid created from four splints of rye straw, the only cereal grown in the region at that time. Schinhats were made by farmers' wives for the family, as protection against the sun. Gradually a modest hat trade started, first between neighbouring villages and then further afield. Gradually, straw was accepted by the fashion houses of Europe, and the hat braiding industry grew into an international trade.

However, as interest developed, other types of straw were used to make braids. Wheat straw was found to be much shinier than rye, and it made an attractive plait. Hats made from this cereal became the height of fashion and rye could not compete.

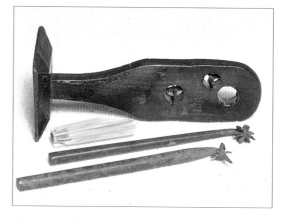

Antique tools used to split straw stems into the narrow splints which were used to make decorations similar to those described in this book. The modern versions of these tools are shown on page 24.

Out of necessity, the Swiss had to look at other ways to use their straw working skills. The local rye was extremely strong, even when split into very narrow strips (splints), and had been used to make straw hat ornaments and decorations. Then, in 1840, the thread wheel was invented – this was a hand-operated, straw-twisting machine which turned flat splints into an extremely strong straw thread.

The local traders, their wives and the cottage industry workers, now used their

Antique straw lace braids – a page from a travelling salesman's sample catalogue. All six braids are variations of a basic design – from the top downwards: the basic design; with additional synthetic material motifs; with straw splint motifs; with straw buttons; with pairs of straw buttons; and, lastly, with straw spreuer motifs.

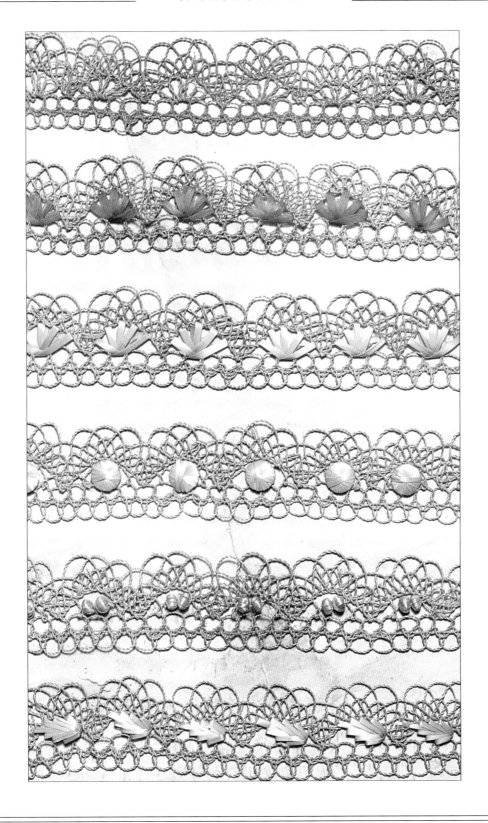

A selection of 19th century borders. From the top: an embroidered wheel braid; a border woven on a wooden handloom – the warp was usually silk and the weft included straw thread, horsehair, straw splints and other materials; a bobbin lace border made with horsehair and decorated with straw; a knotted macramé braid made with straw thread.

ingenuity and skills to design a unique range of beautiful knotted straw thread hats and ornaments. These soon became fashionable and sought after, and this type of Swiss straw work started to flourish.

Then, very gradually, the market for handmade braids and decorations started to wane. In the latter half of the nineteenth century, new synthetic materials became available which could be worked on machines. Factories were built to supply the demands of an ever-changing fashion industry. The factories continued to produce large quantities of synthetic straw braids and other hat-making materials through the twentieth century. However, fashions change and, during the 1950's, hats suddenly began to lose their appeal. The demand for the products declined, and factories rapidly began to close.

I am fortunate to have as a friend, J. Rudolf Isler, a direct descendant of Jacob Isler who, together with a few partners, started the first Swiss straw trading company in 1787. The business prospered and traded for over two hundred years until it finally closed, the last of its kind, in 1991.

J. Rudolf Isler was also one of the members of the commission which founded the Wohlen Straw Museum. It was the visit to this wonderful institution that instilled in me a love of Swiss straw work. I hope that this book will inspire you, and fill you with the same passion.

An antique vesta case (used to hold matches), decorated with straw marquetry.

OVERLEAF:
A collection of antique Swiss straw work. The produce of a thriving cottage industry during the late-nineteenth and early-twentieth centuries.

This antique doily is created entirely from straw. The knotted work is twisted straw thread, and fourteen straw splint spreuers decorate the outer edge. Instructions for making a similar doily are given on page 66.

Six families worked together to create this beautiful ornamental straw tablecloth which was exhibited at the 1855 World Trade Fair in Paris. It includes all the motifs that were known at that time, and they were stitched together using horse hair.

Preparing the straw

Straw is the stem of cereal crops such as wheat, oats, rye and barley, and is essentially a waste product of the grain industry. In order to reduce the amount of straw generated, modern varieties of these cereals have been bred to grow short, stocky stems. Some of these types can be used for Swiss straw work, but you will find that the older varieties, with their long hollow stems, are much better. Straw is a natural fibre and will keep in good condition for many years if you store it in a dry place.

Before you can start any of the projects in this book you must first prepare the straw. In this chapter I show you how to cut the stems into useable lengths, how to grade it to size and then how to make it flexible enough to work with.

All varieties of straw are basically the same colour – albeit in a rather wide shade range – so I have included instructions for creating your own range of colours by dyeing the straw.

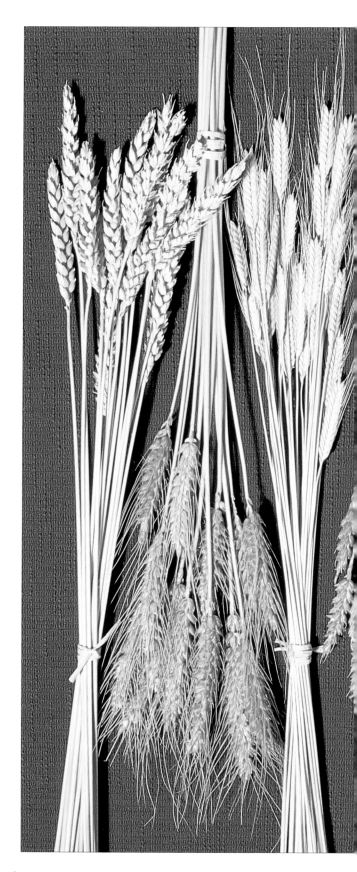

A selection of cereals that provide useable straw. From the left: Maris Widgeon wheat, Red Bearded Wheat, Einkorn Wheat, Square Head Master Wheat, Elite le Purple Wheat, Club Wheat, Emmer Wheat, Black Persian Wheat, Black Oats.

Tools and materials

The equipment needed to prepare the straw is shown in the photograph below. For cutting and soaking the straw, you will need a sharp pair of scissors, a large container in which to soak a batch of cut straw lengths and a damp tea towel. For colouring straw, you will need boil-in dyes, table salt and a stainless-steel pan for boiling the straw (a friend made the one below for me but an old fish kettle would work well). You will also need some weights (I use pebbles and pieces of masonry) to hold the straw down, a pair of plastic gloves and a stick to help lift out the dyed straw.

Tools and materials for preparing straw:
1. Scissors
2. Tea towel
3. Weights
4. Stainless-steel pan
5. Plastic container
6. Plastic gloves
7. Boil-in dyes
8. Wooden stick
9. Salt.

Cutting and grading straw

Each stem of cereal comprises a stalk with two nodes (leaf joints) and a seed head. The nodes are short, solid pieces of stalk which must be cut away and discarded along with the leaves and the seed head. The short base length of stalk is normally unusable and must be discarded. Some cereal stems will give more than two lengths of workable straw.

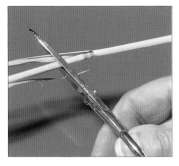

1. Cut off the seed head then cut the stalk 15mm (½in) above and below each node.

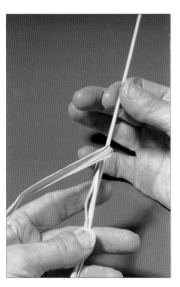

2. Carefully pull the leaves off the workable lengths of straw.

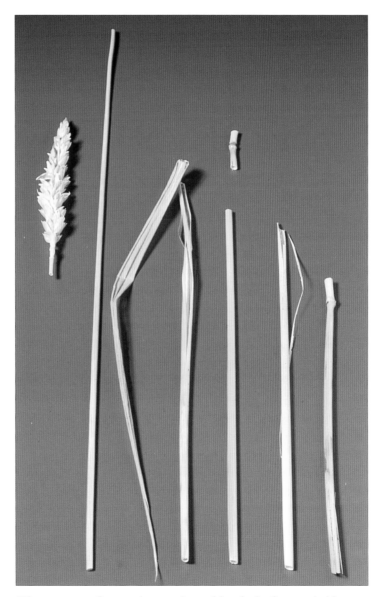

The segments of a cereal stem: the seed head, the first workable straw, the first leaf, the first node, the second workable straw, the second leaf and the base with the second node.

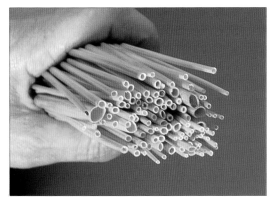

3. Continue cutting workable lengths of straw. A straw stem tapers from the base to the seed head, and individual stems are slightly different in diameter. Therefore, you will find lots of sizes in a batch of cut straws.

4. I generally grade the straw into three separate bundles – large, medium and small diameters – but you can be more particular if you wish.

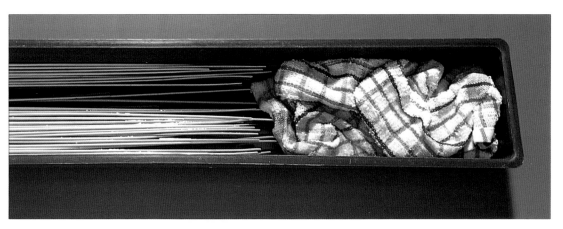

5. Dry straw is very brittle, so when you are ready to start working, soak a batch of cut straw and a tea towel in warm water for approximately twenty minutes.

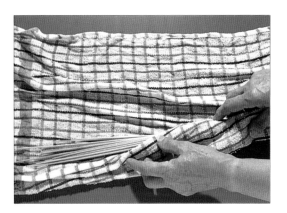

6. Remove the straw stems from the trough and wrap them in the wet towel for at least ten minutes. This will mellow them, and make them more pliable and easier to work with.

> **Tip** If you want to colour straw, soak it in mordant solution of 50% ammonia and 50% water, instead of plain water, before dyeing it. Read the manufacturer's instructions on the ammonia container.

Colouring straw

Straw has a silicone coat on the outside which means that the colour has to be added by boiling the dye into the straw. Follow the dye manufacturer's instructions and protect your hands with a suitable pair of plastic gloves. I use boil-in dyes that work best with a saline solution of salt and water. Cold water dyes will not work with straw.

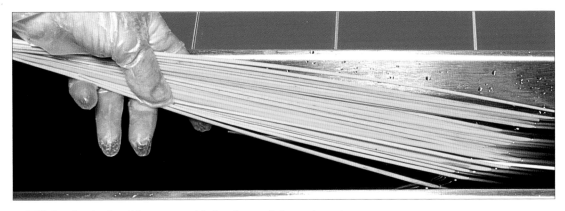

1. Fill the dye bath with water, add the dye and then place the bath on a heat source. Immerse the damp cut lengths of straw into the dye bath.

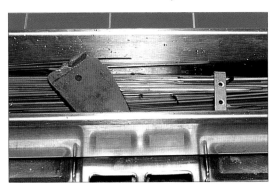

2. Place some weights on top of the straw to stop it floating. Bring the dye up to temperature, add the salt and boil the straw for twenty minutes, then turn off the heat.

3. When the dye solution is cool enough, remove the dyed straw from the dye bath. Rinse it thoroughly in cold water, then spread it out on newspaper to dry. Store the dried straw in a box in a dry area.

Swiss straw work

This chapter shows you how to make a whole range of pretty shapes which can then be used to create geometric patterns, floral displays and a range of jewellery. There are two basic types of Swiss straw work: one type is worked with flat straw splints, the other with twisted straw thread.

In the first part of this chapter I show you how to use straw splints to make spreuers. This is a general name given to a range of leaf-like shapes which are made by winding damp straw splints between the teeth of coarse combs. I also show you how to make rosettes and how to use splints to cover buttons.

In the second part of the chapter I show you how to make straw thread, and then how to use the thread to create a host of different designs. Most of these are 'woven' through a set of needles, but there are also designs that are worked by knotting the thread.

Swiss straw work can be used to create a multitude of shapes, some of which are shown here. Instructions for making all these shapes are included on the following pages.

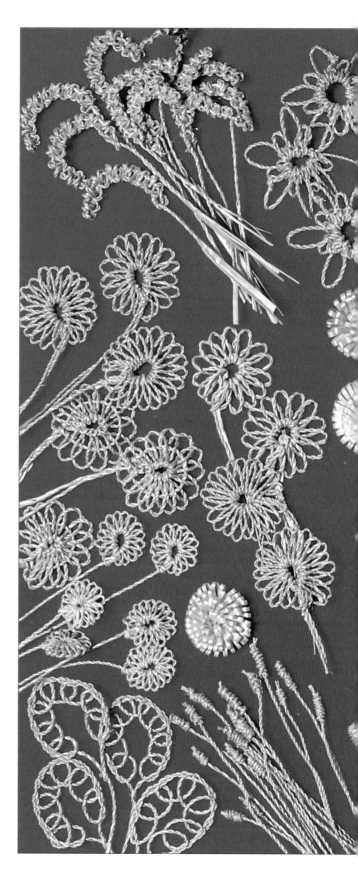

WORKING WITH SPLINTS

Preparing splints

Splints are prepared by first cutting a straw tube into flat strips using either a special splitting tool or a craft knife. These strips are then milled to turn them into very flexible splints. Milling is the most important part of Swiss straw work. Originally, a splint mill would have been used to squash and crush the straw. The mill had two wooden roller turned by a handles and a screw block for tension. However, for the projects in this book hand milling, where the splints are drawn across the closed blades of a pair of scissors to remove the pith, will suffice.

Splitting tools

There are a number of different splitting tools available. They all use the same cutting method; a central pin locates in the end of the straw tube and a set of small blades splits the tube into flat splints. Alternatively, you can cut splints by hand using a craft knife and a cutting mat.

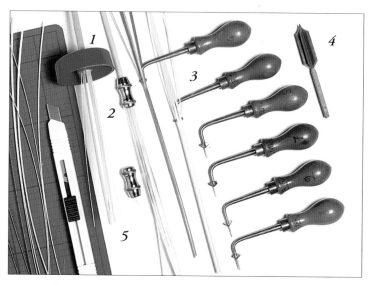

Straw splitting equipment:
1. *Plastic doughnut splitter*
2. *Brass barrel splitter*
3. *Steel point splitters*
4. *Plastic torpedo splitter*
5. *Craft knife and cutting mat.*

Using a splitting tool

The width of a splint will depend on the diameter of the straw tube and the number of blades fitted to the splitting tool. For this example, I have used a six segment, plastic torpedo splitter.

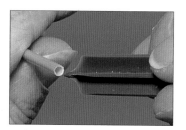

1. Locate the central point of the splitter in the widest end of a damp straw.

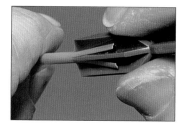

2. Then, carefully push the splitter into the straw.

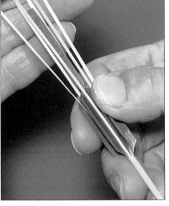

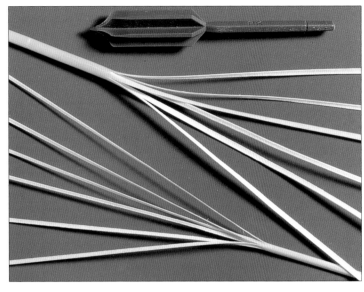

3. When the splitter is fully engaged in the tube, turn the straw and then pull the splitter right through. Keep the central point in the middle of the tube to maintain even width splints.

Use the same splitting tool with different diameter straws to make a range of splint widths.

Using a craft knife
You can also use a craft knife to cut splints. With a little practise, you will soon be able to cut straw tubes into sets of even-width splints.

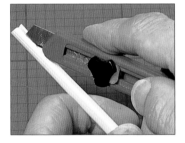

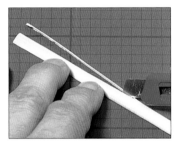

1. Carefully slide the blade of a craft knife down through one side of a length of straw keeping the cut as parallel as possible to the grain.

2. Open out the straw and lay it, pith side down, on a cutting mat. Cut the flattened straw in half, then cut each half into splints of equal width.

Milling splints
There are two sides to a straw splint: the shiny grain side and the dull pith side. For the purposes of the projects in this book, milling involves removing the pith from the 'inside' surface of the splints to make them more pliable.

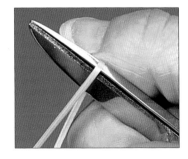

Pull a damp splint, pith side down, over the edge of a closed pair of scissors to remove the pith. Repeat the action a number of times to remove all the pith before starting to work the splint.

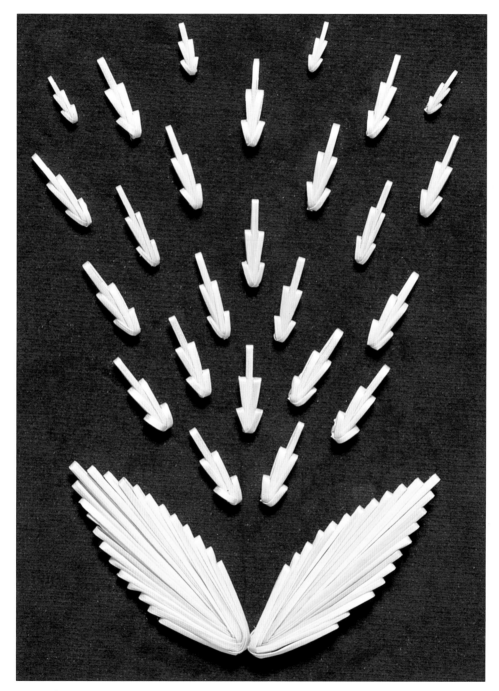

A simple geometric design worked with basic spreuers.

Making spreuers

Spreuers are leaf-like shapes made by winding damp, milled straw splints, shiny side up, between the teeth of a comb. On the following pages I show you, step by step, how to make a basic symmetrical spreuer. When you have mastered this shape, you can try the other designs. You could also experiment, and try making up your own designs.

Tools

Originally, spreuers were worked between a series of headless nails fixed in a piece of wood. Nowadays however, metal dog combs are available, and these are excellent for making straw splint spreuers. Some of these combs have different teeth spaces at either end, and they can be cut in half with a small hacksaw to make them easier to handle.

I paint numbers alongside the teeth on my combs and I refer to them in the step-by-step instructions. In these instructions, a reference to going *over,* say, tooth 6, means that you should take the splint between teeth 6 and 7. A reference to going *under* tooth 6 means that you should take the splint between teeth 5 and 6.

Dog combs are excellent tools for making spreuers.

> **Tip** Paint numbers against the teeth on both sides of the comb, and number each side from opposite ends. This way, while you are waiting for the first spreuer to dry, you can work on a second one at the other end of the comb.

Basic spreuer

Most spreuers are best made on fine combs as the straw does not slip as much as it does on wide ones. However, in this exercise I have used a wide toothed comb to show you the moves more clearly. Mill damp splints two or three times (see page 25) before starting to make spreuers.

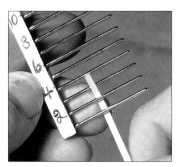

1. Lay the end of a damp, milled splint, pith side uppermost, between teeth 2 and 3.

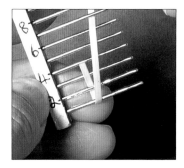

2. Bring the splint up over tooth 1 and then slide it down between teeth 6 and 7.

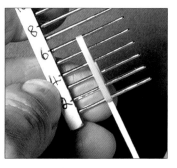

3. Square up the splint, pull it down the back of the comb and bring it up centrally under tooth 1.

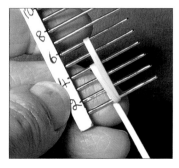

4. Now work to the left of the centre strip and take the splint over tooth 4, down the back and bring it up centrally under tooth 1.

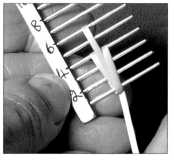

5. Repeat step 4 but work to the right of the centre strip. Centralise the strips at the base of the design (tooth 1).

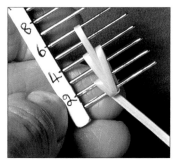

6. Work to the left of the central strip again and take the splint over tooth 2, down the back and up centrally under tooth 1.

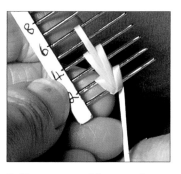

7. Repeat step 6 but work to the right of the centre strip to complete the basic shape.

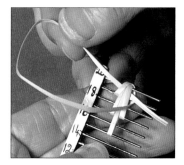

8. At the back of the comb, take the splint across the back of the spreuer and pass it through the bottom loops of the spreuer.

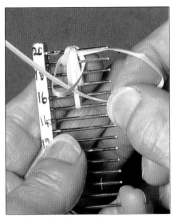

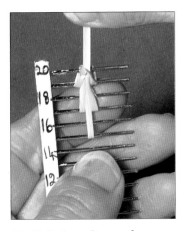

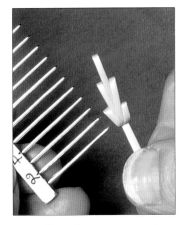

9. Pull the splint to leave a small loop and then pass the end of the splint under and back through this loop.

10. Pull the splint to form a tight, flat knot.

11. Allow the spreuer to dry completely, then carefully slide it off the comb.

Tip When making large spreuers you will need to use more than one splint. Tie off the used up length at the back of the piece, insert a new length into the knot and then pull the knot tight. Continue working the design, adding new lengths as necessary. Make a final flat knot at the bottom of the piece.

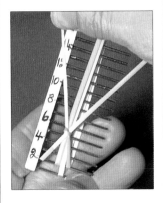

Variations of the basic spreuer. These were made by taking the splint round successive teeth of the comb rather than alternate ones.

Variations of the basic spreuer (see pages 28–29) arranged in a geometric pattern.

Three different sizes of fleur de lys are used to create this geometric design.

Fleur de lys

This variation is made in much the same way as the basic spreuer on pages 28–29, working loops symmetrically either side of a centre strip. However, for this design the splint is wound right round each tooth of the comb before returning to the bottom tooth 1.

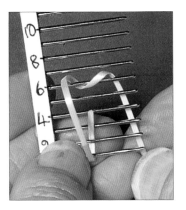

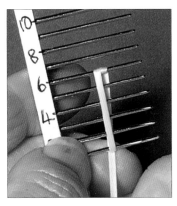

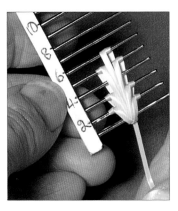

1. Lay the end of a damp, milled splint between teeth 2 and 3. Take the other end over tooth 6, and then wrap it once round tooth 6.

2. Pull the splint down the back of the comb and bring it up centrally under tooth 1. Note that the twist round tooth 6 lays to the right of the central strip.

3. Continue wrapping the splint round successive teeth of the comb. In this example, I worked the left- and right-hand sides of teeth 5, 3 and 2. Finish with a flat knot on the back.

Work the splint round different combinations of teeth to produce variations of the fleur de lys spreuer.

Veined leaf

This delicate little shape is best made on a fine toothed comb. Winding the straw splint round every tooth of the comb will create a good shape.

This spreuer is not symmetrical and you can adjust the final shape by working with different widths of splints.

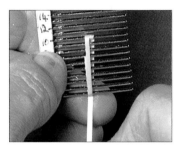

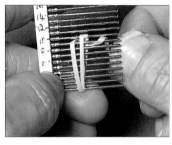

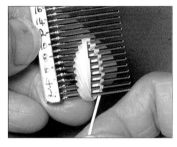

1. Lay a damp, milled splint between teeth 2 and 3. Bring it up under tooth 1 and take it down over tooth 10. Wrap the splint under and over tooth 10 and bring it down the back to tooth 1.

2. Bring the splint up the front and take it down over tooth 9, to the left of the first strip. Now take the splint across the back of the comb and then wrap it under and over tooth 9 to the right of the centre strip.

3. Bring the splint down the back to tooth 1 and then repeat step 2 on tooth 8. Repeat steps 2 and 3 until you reach tooth 2. Bring the end of the splint down the back to tooth 1.

4. Make a finishing knot (see pages 28–29) and leave the leaf on the comb until it is completely dry.

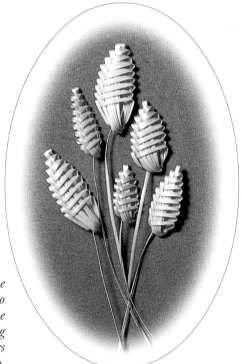

You will need to turn over the woven spreuer to see the actual veined leaf pattern. Notice how I have been able to make both wide and narrow leaves. The shape of these leaves has also been varied by adjusting the weaving pattern; some have been worked round every tooth, others have been stopped short of the bottom of the comb.

Butterfly wings

This pretty spreuer is worked in a similar way to the fleur de lys on page 31 except that the splint is worked on just one side of centre. Work this design on a fine comb to achieve a more rounded shape. As usual, lay a damp, milled splint between teeth 2 and 3 and bring it up under tooth 1 to start this design.

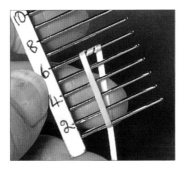

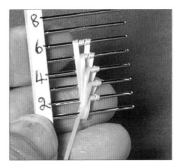

1. Take the splint down over tooth 6 and then wrap it round tooth 6 twice, to the right of centre. Bring the splint down the back and up under tooth 1.

2. Work down the comb wrapping the splint round each successive tooth. Finish with a flat knot (See pages 28–29).

Tip Reinforce the tail end of the spreuer splints with fine wire to help you make a three-dimensional floral display.

Pass a length of fine copper wire through the base loops of a spreuer. Twist the two ends of the wire together. Dampen the splint and start to wrap it round the twisted wire. When the stem is long enough, secure the splint by wrapping the wire round its end two or three turns.

A selection of butterfly wing spreuers.

Floral design made using variations of the basic spreuer, fleur de lys, butterfly wings, veined leaves and covered buttons (see opposite).

Wrapping formers

You can wrap rough wooden buttons and straight formers with damp straw splints to make discs, balls and fancy rosettes.

There are no special items required for wrapping buttons, but you will need a former and two thicknesses of brass wire for the rosettes. Brass wire is used as it is not affected by the moisture in the damp straw; steel wires could become rusty.

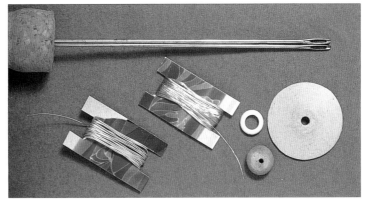

A rosette former (two long candle-wicking needles stuck into a cork), 32 and 24 gauge brass wire and a few button shapes. You can also use other formers (see page 39) to create a range of rosette shapes.

Covering a button

You can cover lots of different blank buttons by wrapping them with damp straw splints. Small buttons will require nimble fingers, but the effort is worthwhile.

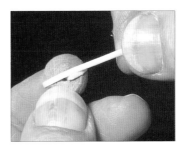

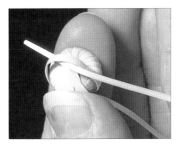

1. Insert a damp splint through the hole in the back of the button. Then take the splint around the button and bring it back over the hole.

2. Continue winding the splint round the button, overlapping each layer. When the button is completely covered, take the end of the splint through the last loop and pull it tight to finish off. When the straw is completely dry, snip off the excess splint.

A selection of straw covered buttons. Leave the tail of the splint on some buttons if you intend incorporating them in a floral design.

Making rosettes

Rosettes are made by winding damp straw splints round a long straight former and a length of thick brass wire. Each complete turn of the splint is secured to the wire with fine brass wire. When the finished wrapping is completely dry, it is slid off the former and twisted round itself to form the rosette. For this exercise I am using a simple former made from two candle-wicking needles fixed, side by side, in a cork.

1. Push the two long needles, side by side, into a cork.

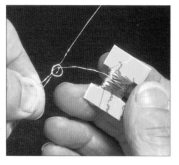

2. Secure one end of a length of thick wire to a firm support (a chair back). Tie a length of fine wire to the other end of the thick wire.

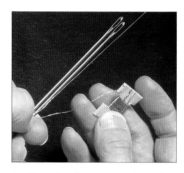

3. Lay the former against the thick wire and, placing your thumb over the wire knot, pull the thick wire taut.

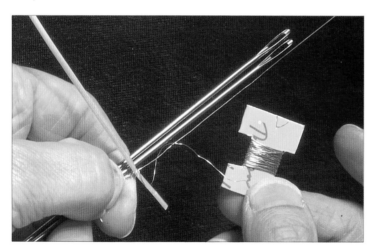

4. Lay the end of a damp splint across both the former and the thick wire. Bind the splint to the thick wire with two turns of the fine wire.

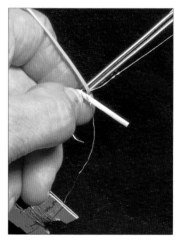

5. Wrap the splint tightly round the former and bring it back over the top.

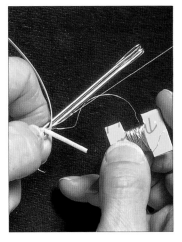

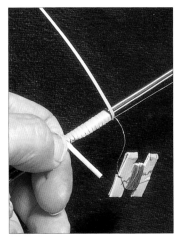

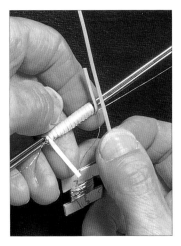

6. Secure the loop to the thick wire by bringing the thin wire up and over the thick wire to the right of the loop. Do not pull the wire too tightly as it may cut through the splint.

7. Continue working up the former repeating steps 5 and 6. Keep the wrapping as tight and as close together as possible.

8. When a splint is used up, lay a new splint over the short end of the first one, anchor it with a turn of fine wire and continue wrapping the new length up the former.

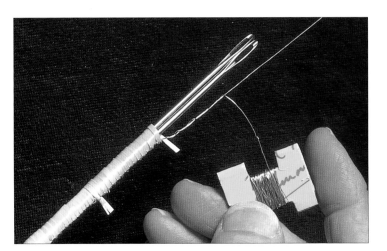

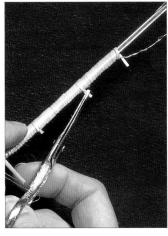

9. When the piece is long enough – a 10cm (4in) length will be sufficient for this rosette – twist the thin wire around the thick wire tightly, four or five times. Trim off the ends of both wires.

10. Use a sharp, pointed pair of scissors to trim the joining flaps down to 3mm ($\frac{1}{8}$in).

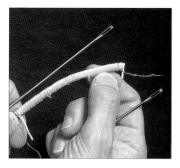

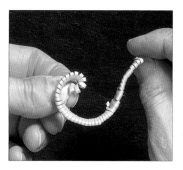

11. Carefully pull one of the needles out of the cork and the wrapping, then slide the wrapping off the other needle.

12. Hold the bottom wire knot in one hand and wind the wrapping around itself in a spiral.

13. Continue winding until you have used up the whole length.

14. Bring the twisted end of the wire down to the knotted end and gently twist all the wires together. Leave the rosette to dry completely, then twist the wire into a stem.

Just a few of the rosettes that you can make. This is one area of Swiss straw work where you can really experiment by trying out different formers.

Other rosette formers

Any stiff, smooth and straight object can be used as a former for making rosettes. The object can also have any cross sectional profile – square, circular, oval, triangular, flat – the choice is yours. Work the rosettes in the same way as the project on pages 36–38, keeping the thick wire against one edge of the former over the whole length of the wrapping.

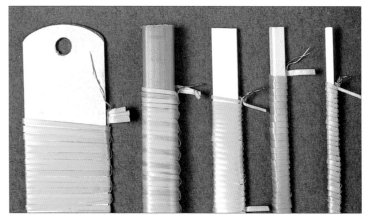

You can use lots of different shapes as formers for rosettes.

Part of a design worked with straw splints, rosettes, covered buttons and basic spreuers.

I used a 12mm (½in) square-section length of plastic as the former for the border, and I wrapped two splints together, side by side.

I used a very thin length of plastic, 12mm (½in) wide, for the flat rosettes in the corners.

I tied two No. 12 knitting needles together to make the former for all the other rosettes.

I covered four 10mm (³⁄₈in) diameter flat wooden buttons for the straw balls round the central rosette.

I couched straw splints to the backing fabric with silk thread.

The lovely leaf-like spreuers can be used to create pretty pairs of earrings.
The larger ones can be transformed into elegant brooches.

WORKING WITH THREADS

Making straw threads

Twist two damp and thoroughly milled lengths of straw splints together and you have a strong thread. This can be used to make a wide range of designs which will add a new dimension to your straw work. Rye is the best cereal to work with as it is very strong. It also has long stems from which you can make good working lengths of thread.

However, lengths of straw thread can be joined together using a weaver's knot (see page 46), so you do not have to worry about length. Special machines for twisting threads are available, but I like to improvise by using a hand drill or by twisting lengths of straw splints by hand.

Twisting threads with a hand drill

You need a hand drill, a pair of clamps, two lengths of string, two 60g (2oz) weights, two angle brackets (to act as guides) and three stiff wire hooks.

The hooks are fitted to the drill chuck and to the ends of the lengths of string. The equipment is clamped to a work bench or tabletop as shown overleaf.

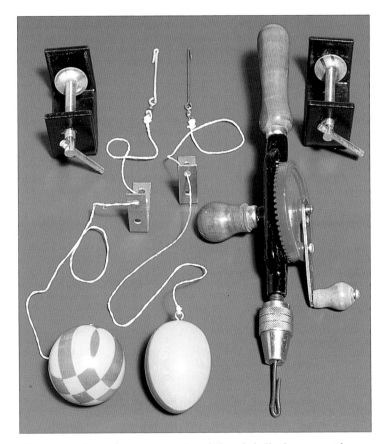

Equipment for twisting straw thread: hand drill, clamps, guides, string, weights and wire hooks.

1. Set the equipment up as shown. Use one clamp to secure the drill in a horizontal position on the table, with its handle on top. Use the other clamp to fix the two guides at the edge of the table. Thread the hooked lengths of string through the guides and fix a weight on the free end of each string. Allow the weights to hang over the side of the table.

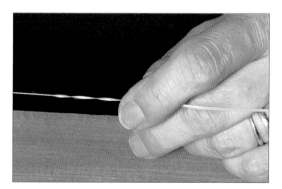

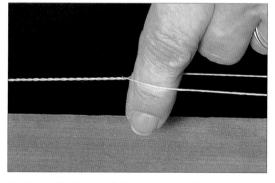

2. Thoroughly mill the damp splints (see page 25) – I suggest you take them over the scissors at least twenty times. Fix a splint to the hook in the drill chuck. Turn the drill handle to twist the splint; slide your fingers along the splint as it twists. Secure the twisted splint to the hook in one length of string. Remove the other end from the chuck, peg it and lay it to one side. Twist another splint in the same way.

3. Now fix both of the twisted splints to the hook in the chuck, and reverse twist them together to make the working thread. Carefully remove the twisted thread from the hooks, peg each end and leave to dry.

Twisting by hand

You can also make a straw thread by twisting damp straw splints by hand. All you need are a few clothes pegs and a weight to hold the ends of the threads. Secure each end of one splint between two pegs, then hold down one end with a weight. Thoroughly twist one splint, peg the end and set aside. Twist a second splint, bring the two twisted splints together and then reverse twist them together to form a thread. This method will take longer than when using the drill but you do have a lot more control over the finished thread. It is also possible to make thicker threads by using more than two splints.

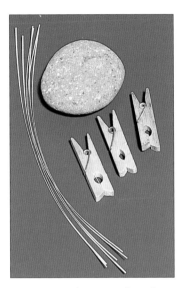

You can make straw threads using just some clothes pegs and a stone weight.

Twisting threads by hand is quite simple and gives you more control over the finished thread.

Using a thread twisting machine

There are a number of special thread twisting machines available which are modern versions of the original design used by the Swiss cottage industry workers. The type shown in use below packs away quite neatly. Each model is slightly different so you must refer to the manufacturer's literature about how to set up and use the machine.

With this particular thread twisting machine you can twist two individual straw splints at the same time. The twisted splints are linked together at the right-hand side and then reverse twisted to complete the thread.

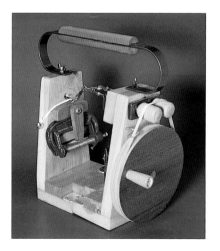

The thread twisting machine shown above, packs away quite neatly.

Weaving with straw threads

Long, joined lengths of straw threads can be woven round needles to form an array of different flower-like shapes. You can also use a knotting technique to produce 'straw lace'. Straw thread has a good matt appearance that contrasts well with the gloss finish of the straw splint spreuers. Combine designs of both types to produce some stunning displays.

Tools and materials

Essentially, you need just two or three needles secured to a piece of wood around which to weave the straw thread. However, the items shown here will help you make all the projects on the following pages.

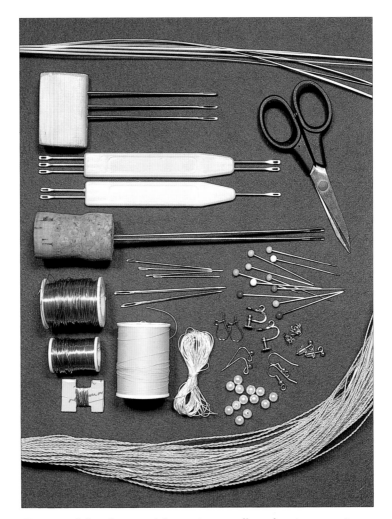

From top left to bottom right: various needle tools, scissors, sewing needles, tapestry needles, dressmaker's pins, brass wire, polyester covered cotton thread, linen thread and jewellery fittings.

Adding thread to a spreuer

This easy technique will give a simple basic spreuer a completely new look.

1. Thread a damp straw thread through the bottom loops of a spreuer, round one of the outer loops and back through the bottom ones.

2. Continue taking the thread round through the remaining loops of the spreuer. Even out the loops either side of the spreuer. Leave to dry and then trim off excess thread.

Three-needle rose

Roses are made by weaving straw thread in a figure-of-eight pattern round three needles. The size of the finished flower is controlled by the distance between each needle, and the number of petals woven. Each complete figure-of-eight weave forms one petal, and the bigger the gap between the needles, the larger the flower. You will need a total length of 60cm (24in) to make this three-needle rose, so you will have to join at least two threads.

1. Join the thin end of two straw threads with a weaver's knot (a sheet bend), close to the ends of the threads.

2. Pull the knot tight and trim the short ends close to the knot.

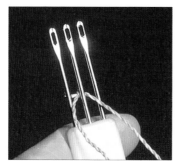

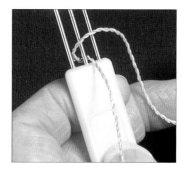

3. Fold the joined threads in half to find the middle point and then loop this over needle 2.

4. Take the left-hand thread over to the right and anchor it at the back of the needle tool with your finger.

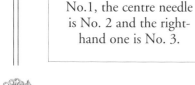

Tip In these step-by-step instructions, needle numbers are allocated from left to right; The left-hand needle is No.1, the centre needle is No. 2 and the right-hand one is No. 3.

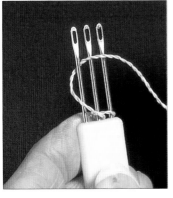

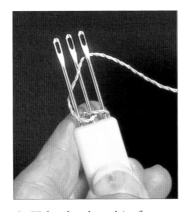

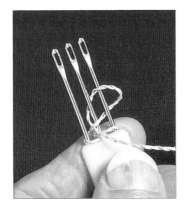

5. Take the other thread across the front of needle 1, round the back and out between needles 1 and 2.

6. Take the thread in front of needle 2 and then back between needles 2 and 3.

7. Bring the thread round in front of needle 3, round the back of needle 2 and back out between needles 1 and 2 to complete the figure-of-eight.

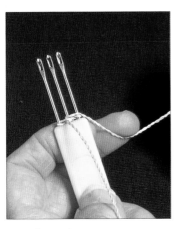

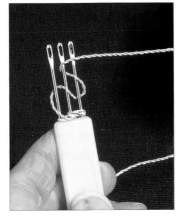

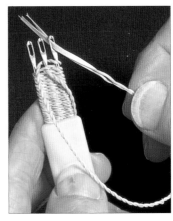

8. Release the resting straw thread. Pull the working thread tight and then anchor it at the back of the needle tool with your finger.

9. Make another figure-of-eight with the new working thread (repeat steps 5–7).

10. Repeat steps 8 and 9 until you have woven eighteen figures-of-eights. Take the end of the working thread 15mm (¹/₂in) through the eye of needle 3.

TIP   If you have unequal lengths of straw thread, make sure that the knot is worked behind needle 2 or 3. This part of the weaving will be at the centre of the finished rose, so the knot will be lost within the mass of thread.

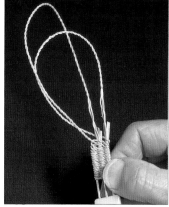

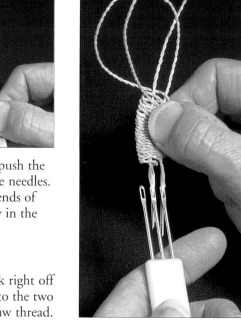

11. Now release the resting thread and pass it through the eye of needle 2.

12. Gently start to push the finished piece off the needles. Make sure that the ends of the straw thread stay in the eyes of the needles.

13. Slide the work right off the needles on to the two long loops of straw thread.

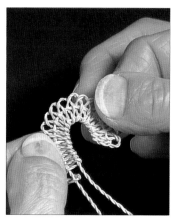

14. Discard the needle tool. Hold the woven piece in one hand, and pull the two ends down until the loops at the top are the same size as those on the woven piece.

15. Ease the woven piece round to form a circle.

16. Pass the inner of the two loose threads, from the back to the front, through the middle loop at the top of the woven piece. In practice, the end of thread may start to unravel as shown here.

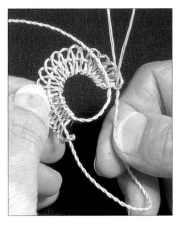

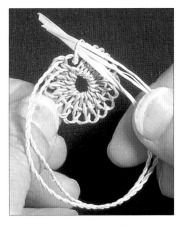

17. Pass the other thread through the outer loop in the same way.

18. Pull the two ends of the woven piece together and then take the ends of both threads down through the first of the woven loops.

19. Pull the threads tight to form a perfect circle. Leave to dry before trimming the ends.

A selection of three-needle roses and two-needle daisies (see page 50).

Two-needle daisy

Daisies are worked using the same basic technique as the rose on pages 48–49, but the straw thread is woven round just two needles rather than three. You can work with the same three-needle tool, but must miss out the middle needle 2. For this exercise I have limited the weaving to fourteen movements to make a more open petal than the rose. You will need a 50cm (20in) length of straw thread.

Tips   If you stop this exercise at the end of step 2, you will have made a two-needle fern.

When closing the woven loop, always take the ends of the threads from the back to the front; this will make the first and last petals overlap correctly.

To make a smaller flower, use a 25cm (10in) length of straw thread and weave round two needles that are close together (for example, two adjacent needles on the three-needle tool).

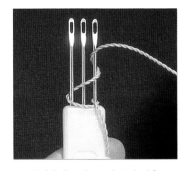

1. Fold the thread in half and loop it over the right-hand needle 3. Anchor the left-hand thread as shown at step 4 on page 46. Take the other thread in a figure-of-eight around needles 1 and 3 as shown, and then pull the thread tight.

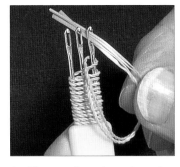

2. Change threads and work another figure-of-eight. Repeat until you have made fourteen movements. Pass the ends of both threads through the eye of needle 3. Push the woven piece off the needle and on to tail ends of the threads.

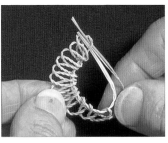

3. Now pass the ends of the threads through the top loop, from the back to the front, and ease the woven piece into a circle.

4. Finally, take the threads through the first woven loop and pull them tight to complete the daisy.

Horseshoe

These shapes can be made as long as you like. They can be decorated with beads as described in this step-by-step project, or they can be left open. The photograph on page 52 shows some of shapes that can be made. Lengths of straw thread are laid in as necessary – they do not have to be knotted. For this exercise you will need two 50cm (20in) lengths and one 10cm (4in) length.

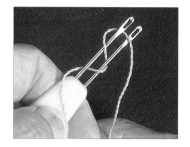

1. Lay a single thread, about 5cm (2in) from one end, over a two-needle tool and work a figure-of-eight around the two needles as shown.

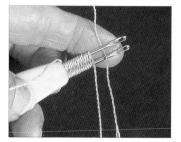

2. Work fourteen rows or up until there is only about 8cm (3in) of the working thread left. Lay this end out to one side (over a needle) and then lay in a new full length of thread beside it.

3. Work another fourteen rows with the second thread, leaving about 8cm (3in) spare before starting to weave. Take 15mm (½in) of the working thread through the eye of the right-hand needle.

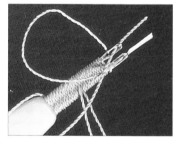

4. Take 15mm (½in) of the 10cm (4in) length of thread through the eye of the left-hand needle.

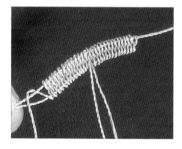

5. Carefully push the work off the needles on to the 10cm (4in) length of thread.

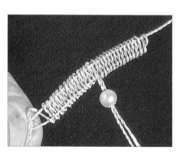

6. Trim the ends off the two threads in the middle of the weaving to make them equal lengths. Thread both ends through a pearl or a bead.

7. Ease the weaving into the shape of a horseshoe. Bring all the ends together and then tie them tightly with sewing thread.

8. Select the best, longest thread as a stem, then trim off all the others close to the base of the horseshoe.

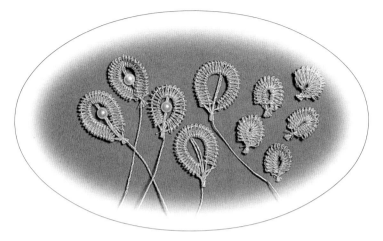

Decorated horseshoes (left) together with a few plain ones (centre) and some smaller ones made with just one length of thread.

Half-hitch fern

The simple, half-hitch knot is very versatile and can be used to make beautiful ferns and a variety of petalled flowers. The technique is worked on a single needle.

1. Tie two equal lengths of thread together (see page 46) and lay the knot in behind the needle.

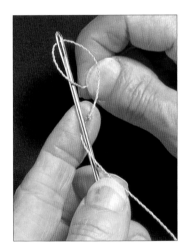

2. Work a half-hitch knot with the right-hand thread.

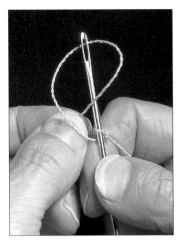

3. Now work a half-hitch knot with the left-hand thread.

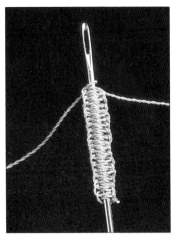

4. Continue making right- and left-hand half-hitches up the length of the needle.

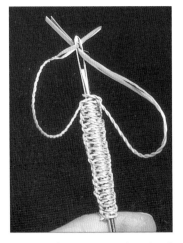

5. Pass about 15mm (½in) of the end of both threads through the eye of the needle.

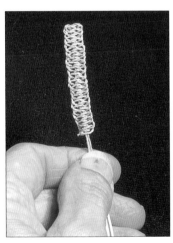

6. Push the weaving off the needle on to the ends of the straw threads. Leave to dry.

Half-hitch ferns. Slide the weaving further down the ends of the straw to make a fern with a more open pattern.

Open half-hitch fern

This fern is made in exactly the same way as the one shown on pages 52–53, except that the knots are tied round two or three needles to form more open loops.

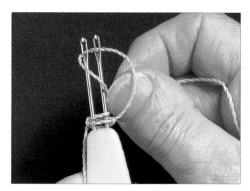

Work open half-hitch ferns over two or three needles as if they were one wide needle.

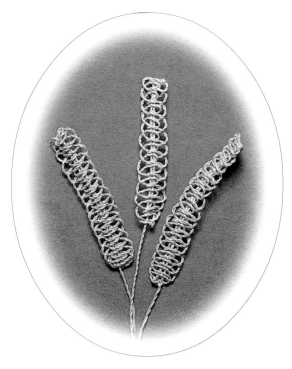

Curly fern

This variation of the half-hitch fern is worked with a single length of straw thread. All the knots are made on one side of the needle with small gaps left between pairs of knots. When the fern is removed from the needle, the mass of straw thread on the knotted side of the work causes it to curl.

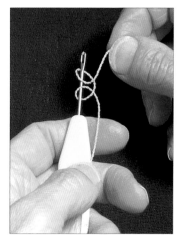

1. Hold an 8cm (3in) tail of a length of straw thread in one hand and then work two opposing half-hitches round a single needle as shown.

2. Pull the knots tight. Place your finger nail just above the first knots and then make another pair of opposite half-hitches, leaving a gap of approximately 3mm ($^{1}/_{8}$in).

3. Continue knotting in the same way up the length of the needle. Pass the end of the thread through the eye of the needle and then pull the weaving off the needle. Tie off the work by taking the start end of the thread, which should be lying at right-angles to the work, through the first loop. Pull the thread tight and leave to dry before trimming off excess thread.

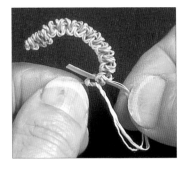

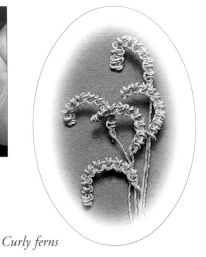

Curly ferns

Buttonhole flowers

This is a variation of the one-needle curly fern above, where the natural curl of the knotting is reversed to create a small open-centred flower.

1. Make a curly fern as steps 1–3 (opposite and above). Then before you tie off the work, reverse the natural curl by pulling the threads at the bottom of the woven piece.

2. When the two ends come together, tie them off by taking the thread through the first hole and then pulling the loop tight. Leave to dry and then trim off the excess straw.

Buttonhole flowers

Two-needle petalled flower

This variation of the curly fern is worked on a two-needle tool. However all the knots are still made round just one needle, but the straw thread is looped round both needles between each pair of half-hitches. Repeat until you have only an 8cm (3in) tail, then take this tail through the eye of the left-hand needle. Push the work off the needles, form it into a circle and take the end of the thread through the loop of the last half-hitch knot.

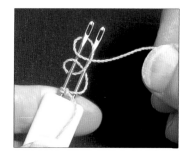

Three-needle petalled flower

Work the technique above on three needles to make flower that have different sizes of petals. Again make all the knots on one needle, but make alternate loops round the other needles; first round the right-hand needle and then round the middle needle.

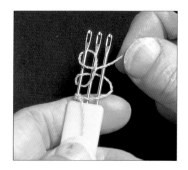

1. Make two knots round the first needle. Loop the thread round the right-hand needle then make another pair of knots round the left-hand needle. As usual, space the knots 3mm (¹/₈in) apart.

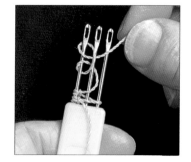

2. Now loop the thread round the middle needle and then make a pair of knots round the left-hand needle. Repeat steps 1 and 2 until your woven piece is the required length and then finish off as described above.

Three-needle and two-needle petalled flowers.

Binding straw threads

Simple binding techniques can be used to create another range of motifs to add to your collection. On the following pages, I show you how to make bulrushes, brooms and carpet beaters.

Bulrushes
For this easy motif, you will need a darning needle, a 5cm (2in) tube of straw and a straw thread.

Bulrushes and mini-bulrushes

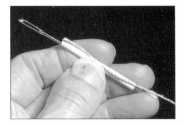

1. Insert a needle through a tube of straw and lay one end of a straw thread along the side of the tube.

2. Work from the bottom of the straw tube and start to bind the straw thread evenly and tightly over the tube and the length of thread.

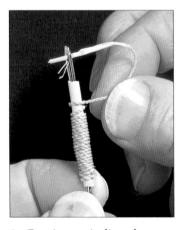

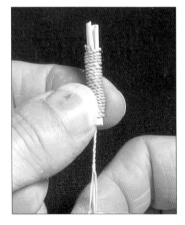

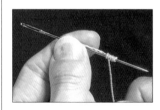

3. Continue winding the thread until there is only 5cm (2in) left and then pass the end of the thread through the eye of the needle.

4. Carefully pull the needle and thread though the tube until the binding is tight – the thread will split the top of the straw tube. Trim the excess straw tube at each end to complete the bulrush.

Tip   You can make miniature bulrushes by omitting the straw tube. When the motif is long enough, pull the end of the thread through the centre of the binding.

Broom

Brooms are made from straw tubes and straw thread. Select a set of narrow diameter tubes that are all the same length.

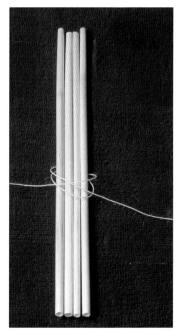

1. Place four straw tubes side by side and tie a loose clove-hitch with sewing thread round the middle of the straws as shown.

2. Pull the knot tight – the straws will splay out – and then secure with a neat knot.

3. Fold up straws at the knot. Pinch the fold tightly and insert a small pin against the inside of the fold.

4. Hold a needle at the back of the work, and then lay a straw thread through the middle of the fan of straws.

5. Change hands and start binding with the straw thread, winding it above the pin, round the fan of straw tubes and the needle.

6. Bind six or seven turns of the straw thread and then pass the end of the thread through the eye of the needle. Pull the needle and thread through the binding to tighten it.

7. Trim off the excess straw thread and then shape the ends of the straw tubes. Leave the pin in place and set the work aside to dry.

A finished broom.

A selection of brooms made with five tubes, not four. Note how you can change the shape by varying the final trim.

Carpet beater – inside loop

Half-hitch knots are used to form this motif. Vary the design by using two or more threads together.

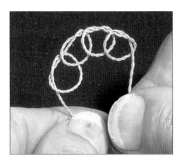

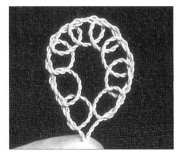

1. Make a loose half-hitch knot, about 5cm (2in) from one end of a length of straw thread. Continue making more loose knots, over-lapping them as shown.

2. When you have made enough knots, bring the two ends of the thread together and secure with fine sewing thread and a neat knot.

Knot two or more threads together to vary this design.

Carpet beater – outside loops

With this version of the carpet beater the loops of the knots are on the outside edge of the carpet beater.

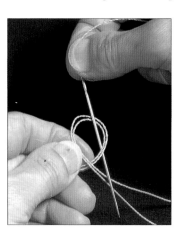

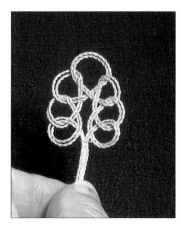

1. Thread two equal lengths of straw thread through a needle, make a loose loop with the other end of the threads and pass the needle through the loop, and over the straw thread, as shown to make an 'outside' loop knot.

2. Make a series of these knots, then bring the two ends together and secure with sewing thread. An odd number of knots will give a central loop to the motif.

You can use the spreuers and straw thread motifs to create simple flower designs.

ABOVE AND RIGHT:
Two simple floral designs created from some
of the motifs described in this book.

This wonderful floral display, which also appears on the cover of this book, includes every type of motif shown in these pages.

Straw lace

The straw lace projects on the following pages are worked in single and double Brussels stitch – traditional stitches commonly used for needle lace. Here I show you, step by step, how to create a small straw lace coaster decorated with spreuers. I then show you how you can add a picot edge to a larger doily.

Coaster

A three-needle rose with sixteen petals (see pages 46–49) is used as the central starting point for this coaster.

1. Make a sixteen petal, three-needle rose. Leave one of the straw threads 10cm (4in) longer than the other.

2. Thread the long thread on a needle and work a single Brussels stitch in the middle of the first petal of the rose.

3. Pull the stitch tight to create the first of another row of loops and then continue to work round the rose in the same way. Join on new threads as necessary with a weaver's knot (see page 46).

4. At the end of the first new row of stitches, trim off the other short straw thread. Now work another row of loops in double Brussels stitch; make the loops slightly larger than the first row.

5. Pull the stitches tight, centralising each in the middle of a lower loop before moving on round the work. Work round until you have worked four complete rows.

6. On the fifth row, add a pair of basic spreuers (see pages 28–29) on to a new loop. Work round this row, adding two spreuers on every fourth loop.

7. On the sixth row work in another spreuer. Take the needle through the centre of the first spreuer, the bottom of the new spreuer and the centre of the third spreuer. Work around this row adding more spreuers in the same way.

8. On the seventh row, take the loop through the middle of the central spreuer. Note how the loops through the spreuers are much bigger than the adjacent loops in the same row.

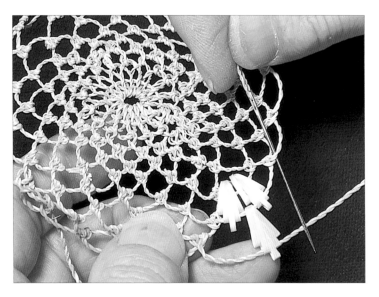

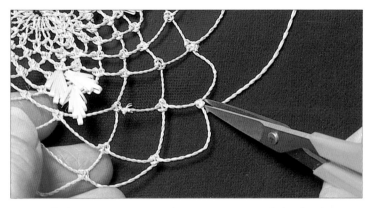

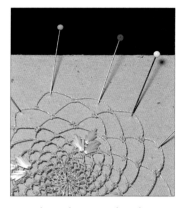

9. Work three more rows without spreuers. End the final row opposite the very first stitch, then trim off the excess thread.

10. Place the completed coaster on a board and pull it into shape. Use pins as shown to hold the shape. Steam the coaster with an iron, then leave to dry.

Doily

Doilies are just large versions of the coaster shown above. For the doily shown opposite, I used a thirty-two petal, three-needle rose as the centre motif, working the first row in single Brussels stitch and the rest in double Brussels stitch. You can enhance the basic design by adding a decorative picot edge round the completed doily.

1. Work the decorative picot edging with fine straw threads. Work six, tight half knots then leave a loop on the next one. Repeat this pattern round the doily edge. Stretch and steam the doily as for the coaster.

2. Add a smaller three-needle rose to the centre of the doily. Slip stitch it into position, working the securing thread through both of the flowers.

The finished coaster.

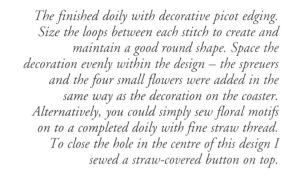

The finished doily with decorative picot edging. Size the loops between each stitch to create and maintain a good round shape. Space the decoration evenly within the design – the spreuers and the four small flowers were added in the same way as the decoration on the coaster. Alternatively, you could simply sew floral motifs on to a completed doily with fine straw thread. To close the hole in the centre of this design I sewed a straw-covered button on top.

Straw Embroidery

Straw has been embroidered on to fabric for many years now, using traditional embroidery stitches. In this chapter I show you how to work with straw splints and straw thread to produce the design opposite, which is based on two early-eighteenth-century pieces at The Victoria and Albert Museum in London, England. Museums are a good source of inspiration, and I have spent many happy hours studying straw embroideries and traditional techniques.

All the stitches and techniques used for this straw embroidery are described on the following pages.

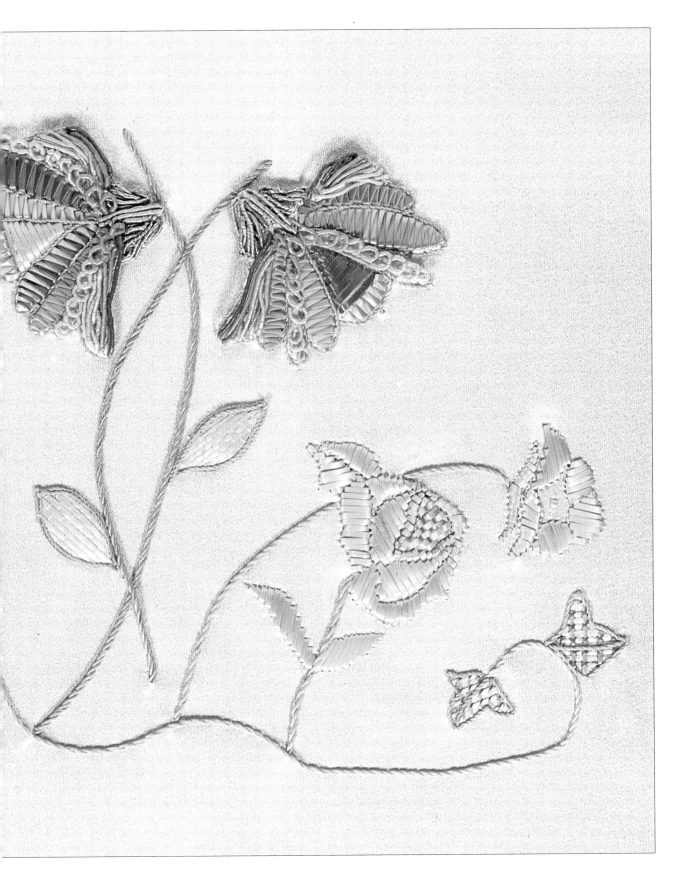

Tools and materials

Apart from the straw splints and straw threads, most of the other items that you will need to complete the project in this chapter will be found in any good needlecraft suppliers.

Fabrics

You can embroider on lots of different fabrics: silk, satin, net, organza, muslin and calico are all good surfaces. However, remember that you will be working with *damp* straw, so test your fabric for water marking before you start. Stains on a completed embroidery will spoil the effect.

Needles

I use a tapestry needle on a soft fabric such as satin; it has a blunt point which separates the fibres of the fabric and allows straw splints to pass through with ease. Sharper needles could split the fibres and this could damage the straw. However, on firmer fabrics such as calico, I use a large crewel needle to make a hole big enough for the splint to pass through unhindered.

Threads

I tend to use just crochet cotton, linen thread and polyester-covered cotton thread. Pure polyester thread is so strong that, if pulled too tightly, it could cut right through the straw.

The tools and materials used for straw embroidery.

Frames

Frames

It is important to stretch the backing fabric used for straw embroidery on a frame. You can use conventional slate frames, embroidery hoops and artists' stretchers. However, I like to keep costs to a minimum, so I use old picture frames. I also ask my husband to make simple frames from scrap pieces of plywood (cut the centre out of a rectangular piece and you have the right shape). If you use home-made frames, I suggest that you stick masking tape round the edges to cover any roughness.

You will need strong thread to lace your fabric on to a slate frame, cotton strips to bind embroidery hoops or a supply of silk pins to stretch the fabric on other types of frame.

Other items

A sharp pair of scissors is an essential for any workbox, and you should have a pencil, tape measure and some tracing paper. I also include a selection of beads, sequins and ribbons to decorate my work, and a good supply of sewing pins. You must keep the straw damp; I keep a finger bowl of water by my side and frequently stroke the straw with wetted finger tips.

You can use all sorts of frame for your straw embroideries.

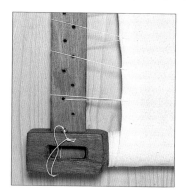

Use a strong linen thread to lace up slate frames so that the fabric is held taut while you work your embroidery.

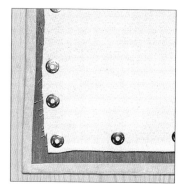

Use silk pins to stretch fabric on other types of frame. Fix the centres of opposite sides of the fabric first, then opposite corners. Finally pin the lengths in between, spacing the pins 4cm (1½in) apart.

Transferring a design

I use tracing paper to transfer my designs on to the fabric. Enlarge the diagram below on a photocopier and then trace the complete design on to the front of the tracing paper with a soft pencil. Turn the tracing paper over and retrace the design to give a pencilled image on both sides.

For this project, I stretched a piece of cream satin on to a home-made frame.

1. Transfer the design from the tracing on to the fabric.

2. Use a sharp pencil to enhance any faint areas of the traced image.

Enlarge this diagram by 200% to make a full size pattern.

Stitches

To complete the project design you will use the following techniques and stitches: raised darning, satin stitch, couching, laidwork, or nué, padded work, wrapping and porcupine quill work. The latter is a technique unique to straw embroidery. Mill straw splints at least ten times (see page 25).

Raised darning

Straw splints are worked on the surface of the fabric, shiny side uppermost, with only the start and finish ends passing through the fabric. The splints lay lengthwise across the widest part of the design. Polyester-covered cotton thread is used to couch damp splints down over lengths of rustproof florist's wire (or needles) laid temporarily at right angles under the splints. On the design, this stitch is used for the centre of the rose.

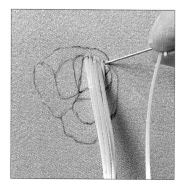

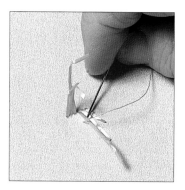

1. Thread a 15cm (6in) damp splint on a tapestry needle. Take the end of the splint through the fabric in the middle of one edge of the petal to be filled. Lay more splints, side by side, across the top of the petal.

2. On the back of the fabric, anchor the ends of the splints with polyester-covered cotton thread. Back stitch each splint separately to secure and then temporarily anchor the rest of this thread on one side. Trim off excess ends of splints.

Tip Keep a small dish of water close by as you work. You can then keep the splints damp while you work with them.

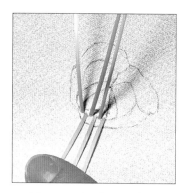

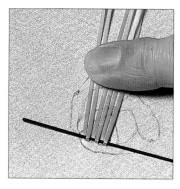

3. Turn to the front of the fabric and separate alternate splints into two groups of three. Fold one group backwards (pith side uppermost).

4. Lay a length of rustproof florist's wire between the two groups of splints, then bring the first group back over the top of the wire.

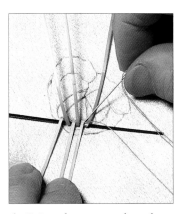

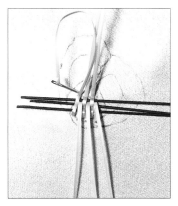

5. Now fold back the second group of splints so they are pith side uppermost.

6. Bring the cotton thread up to the front, close to the side of the right-hand splint of the first group. Take the thread over this first splint and back down close to other side of the splint. Work across to the left-hand side, couching the other splints in the group.

7. Lay in another length of wire between the two groups of splints, fold back the first group and then bring the second group forward over the wire. Repeat step 6 to couch this group to the fabric. Repeat this step, alternating the first and second groups of splints to fill the area. As the petal shape starts to narrow, take the outer splints down through the fabric.

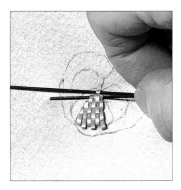

8. Continue working across the image and then take the final splint down through to the back of the fabric.

9. On the back of the fabric, use slip stitch to secure all the straw splints, taking the thread twice over each splint. Trim off all excess ends.

10. Finally, when the straw is completely dry, remove the lengths of florist's wire from under the splints.

Satin stitch

Satin stitch is worked using 15–20cm (6–8in) lengths of straw splints, with the shiny side out and the pith side against the fabric. Here I am using satin stitch to cover the other rose petals. Start sewing at the widest part of the petal to be covered. Work across one side, then come back to the middle and finish the other side of the petal.

1. Thread a damp splint on a needle. Bring the splint up through the fabric on the edge of the design, across the widest part of the petal, then back through the fabric. Ensure that the splint lays flat on the fabric, shiny side up.

2. Continue stitching across one side of the shape. Keep the lengths of sewn splint as close together as possible. When you reach the edge of the shape, take the splint down through the fabric.

Tip Use relatively short lengths of splint when working satin stitch. The straw is passed up and down through the fabric for each stitch, and too much of this action will cause a splint to fragment. However, simple joins allow you to cover large areas.

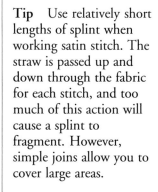

3. On the underside of the fabric, tuck the initial short tail end of splint under the stitches. Take the working splint under the stitches, back to the widest part of the petal, then work the other side of the petal in the same way. Finish by tucking the splint through the stitches on the under side of the fabric and trimming off excess splint.

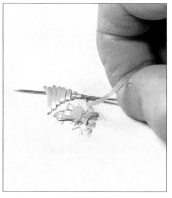

4. Repeat steps 1–3 for the other petals and leaves. Change the grain of the stitch on each petal to separate them from each other and so create a realistic flower. The stems are couched with sewing thread (see opposite).

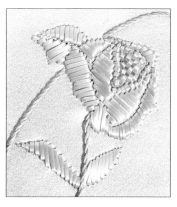

Couching

I use this technique for flower stems and tendrils. Straw threads are tapered, very much like the stems they will represent, so couch them down accordingly. Always use a length of straw thread at least 5cm (2in) longer than the design. Take both ends down through the fabric and, when the thread has been couched down, trim excess threads and oversew the short ends. Use sewing thread, the same shade as the straw to couch the straw to the fabric. Again, remember that straw thread must be dampened before you embroider with it.

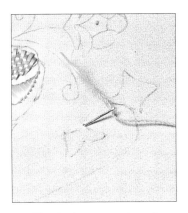

1. Check the straw thread length against the pattern, then take the ends down through the fabric to leave short tails at each end.

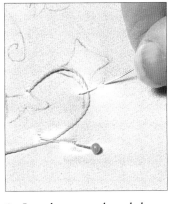

2. Lay the straw thread down on the fabric, following the curves of the stem design, and temporarily pin the straw thread to the fabric.

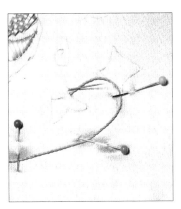

3. Using straw coloured cotton thread, knot the end and bring the thread up close to the end point of the stem.

4. Take the cotton thread over the straw, following the natural twist of the straw, and back down through the fabric; pull the sewing thread so that it falls naturally into a groove in the straw thread. In this enlarged photograph I have deliberately left the sewing thread visible. Continue couching the stem, placing the stitches at 5mm (¼in) intervals.

Laid work

Straw splints can be laid on the surface of the fabric, in vertical and horizontal rows, to create a laid work pattern. On this design I use the technique to embroider some leaves. Always start with the longest length and work outwards in one direction to create an even design. Work the first set of splints leaving a space, equal to the width of the splints, between each one.

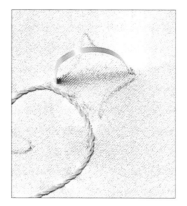

1. Use a tapestry needle to pull a damp splint up through the fabric at the base of the leaf. Take it across the leaf and back down through the fabric. Pull the stitch tight, leave a space equal to the width of a splint, then work more stitches across the leaf, parallel to the first stitch.

2. Now work another set of stitches over, and at right angles to, the first set.

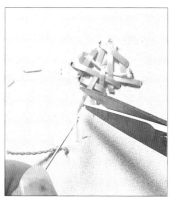

3. On the back of the fabric, thread the tail end of the splints under the stitches and trim excess ends.

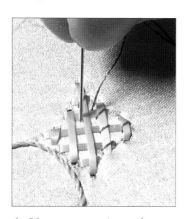

4. Use a contrasting colour of embroidery thread to secure the straw splints to the fabric. Sew a series of stitches, all in the same direction, across the diagonal of each intersection.

5. Now use the same thread to make another series of stitches across the opposite diagonals of the splints to form neat X-shaped stitches. Complete the leaf by couching a straw thread round its edge.

Or nué

This traditional goldwork technique works very well with the rich golden colour of straw. Use straw-coloured sewing thread to couch the splints to the fabric. These stitches must be spaced very evenly, so I prefer to work a design on an open weave, silk gauze where I can count the holes. I then cut round the shape and couch it to the fabric, together with a straw thread edging. I use this technique for the two central leaves on the pattern.

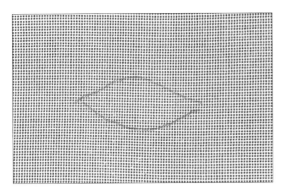

1. Trace a leaf on to the silk gauze, aligning its two points along the grain of the gauze.

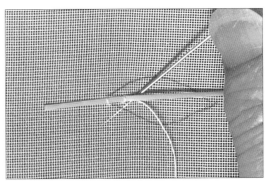

2. Lay a straw splint on the gauze parallel to the grain. Couch the splint to the gauze with sewing thread, keeping the stitches within the drawn outline. Use the holes in the gauze to space each stitch evenly along, and at right angles to, the splint. Trim each end of the splint just beyond the drawn outline.

3. Lay another straw splint alongside the first and couch this to the fabric. Make these stitches exactly midway between those on the first splint. Continue to couch down more strips until the whole shape is covered. Cut round the outside of the shape, cutting through the ends of the couched splints, and then secure to the main fabric by couching a straw thread round the outside.

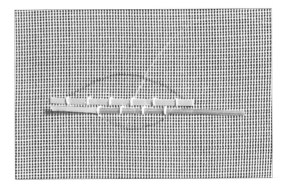

Padded work

Padding adds depth to an embroidery. For the small shapes on this pattern a single layer of felt padding will be enough. For large, high areas layer the padding to give a smooth shape. Sew each layer to the fabric separately, starting with the smallest. This is a good technique to add shape to the centre of the flowers on the pattern.

1. Cut a piece of felt padding, slightly smaller than the area to be padded, and slip stitch it into place with cotton thread.

2. Use satin stitch (see page 76) to cover the design; take the splints over the padding, across the widest part of the design.

Porcupine quill work

Porcupine quill work is a technique that is unique to strawcraft, and was used extensively on eighteenth-century straw work. Colour plays a very important part in the technique and it is best worked with contrasting colours of straw.

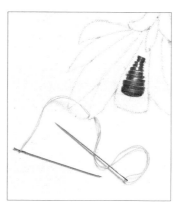

1. Thread two needles with cotton threads that tone with the straw splints (pink in one needle, a natural colour in the other). Knot the ends and bring the threads up through the fabric one splint width down from the tip of the petal. For this exercise bring the pink thread up on the left-hand side).

2. Thread the narrow ends of two contrasting splints, pith sides together, on a third needle. Work with uneven lengths of splints so that one runs out before the other. Take the splints down through the fabric, with the red splint facing to the right. Leave short ends on the underside – these will be covered as you work the stitches.

3. Fold the two splints down to the left of the petal as shown (red splint on top) and use the pink cotton to backstitch them into place. Bring the pink cotton back up to the front of the fabric, on the outline of the petal, leaving a gap equal to the width of one splint.

4. Now fold the splints across to the right (natural splint on top) and use the straw-coloured cotton to backstitch them into place. Again, bring the cotton back up to the front of the fabric, on the outline of the petal, leaving a gap equal to the width of one splint.

5. Repeat steps 3 and 4, following the outline of the petal. Work until a short end is left on the top splint, then trim it so that it will lay just short of the full width of the petal.

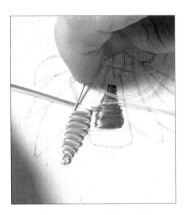
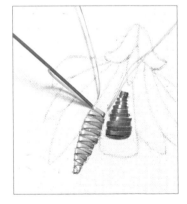

6. Select a new splint, the same width and colour as the short end beneath. Lay it over the short end, on top of the folded-down natural splint, and backstitch with the pink thread.

7. Trim the end of the new red splint, one-third of the width of the design, away from the last backstitch. Fold the splints back, check that the short end of the red splint is not visible, then backstitch the splints in the usual way.

8. Continue working until you reach the end of the petal, then take both threads to the back of the fabric. Trim the splints to the same length and take them down to the back. Oversew the ends using the cotton thread.

Wrapping

This technique involves wrapping a damp straw splint round a length of thread. You can vary the weight of the wrapping by using different thicknesses of thread. The wrapped lengths of thread can then be shaped and secured to the fabric. On the pattern, some of the shapes are covered with the curled, wrapping shown in the step-by-step instructions. Others are covered with straight wrapping as shown at the bottom of the page.

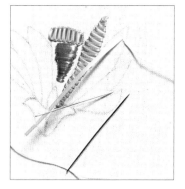

1. Thread a damp straw splint in one needle and cotton thread in another. Take both needles through the fabric, through the same hole, and oversew the tail end of the splint.

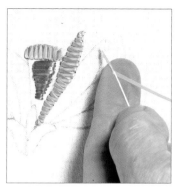

2. On the front of the fabric, pull the cotton thread taut and wrap the splint, pith side innermost, round the thread for about 15mm (½in).

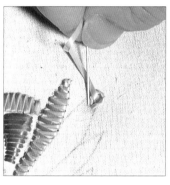

3. Form a small loop with the wrapped thread as shown, then take the thread and splint back through the fabric close to the first hole.

4. Hold the loop flat with a pin and then bring the splint and cotton thread back to the front of the fabric, a little way down from the first loop.

5. Repeat steps 2 and 3 down the length of the area to be filled, overlapping the loops and varying their size to fit the width of the shape. Move the pin down the design to hold the lowest loop. Remove the pin when the straw is completely dry.

Tip Use a similar technique, but without forming loops, to make long straight wrappings for the green calyx of the flowers.

Embroidering on net

Straw is so light in weight that it can even be worked on flimsy materials such as net. If you are careful with the finishing, a design on net can be viewed from both sides. You can couch splints, weave spreuers and apply other straw thread motifs to create beautiful designs.

Couching

Lay the stretched net over a design and 'couch' long stems into place by weaving the straw thread through the net.

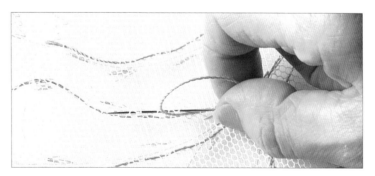

Weaving spreuers

The open structure of net allows you to weave spreuers (see pages 28–29) directly to the surface of the net. If you use variations of the basic spreuer your design will be reversible.

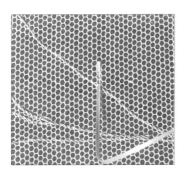
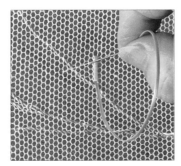
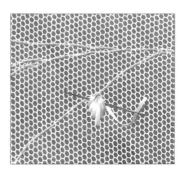

1. Start a spreuer by laying a length of damp straw splint through the holes in the net. For a leaf shape such as this, locate the base of the spreuer close to a couched stem.

2. Weave the spreuer by counting holes in the net instead of the teeth on a comb to create symmetry.

3. When the spreuer is complete, turn the work over and take the tail end of the splint through the back of the spreuer. Carefully trim off the excess splint.

Adding other motifs

You can decorate the surface of the net with lots of other motifs. Many of the straw thread designs shown in this book can be used. For reversible images, select two same sized motifs and couch them, back-to-back, with cotton thread.

Reversible net embroideries can be made into pretty mobiles. All the motifs on this one are worked through the net. The design was taken from the antique net stole, embroidered circa 1835 (see page 7).

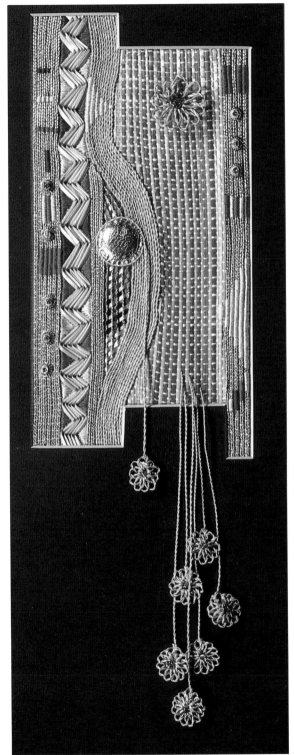

The temptation of straw

I started work on this embroidery at a one-day goldwork course, and managed to complete the three vertical bands of couched gold thread before the day ended. Back at home, while looking for gold threads to continue the piece, I realised that my beloved straw was also golden in colour. Temptation overcame my original desire, and I finished the piece with straw thread and splints. The design built up as follows:

A zig-zag of fairly-open, porcupine quill work, stitched with pale green and natural straw splints.

Couched, vertical bands (the last of my gold thread) are interwoven at an angle with dyed straw splints.

Twisted straw threads, couched with straw coloured cotton thread, create the wide golden band curving through the middle of the design.

The large expanse of 'or nué' is actually alternating strips of red and natural straw splints couched with linen thread.

Two-needle daisies, with very long stems hang from the work. A two-needle daisy, worked on wide needles is sewn to the or nué piece.

A detail of the design showing, from the left, porcupine quill work, a band of gold thread, gold thread interwoven with coloured straw splints, a curved band couched straw thread and the straw 'or nué' work.

Waterfall

Inspiration for the waterfall came from HRH Princess Margaret's 21st. birthday gown, designed by Christian Dior in 1951.

Natural raffia knots and loops form focal points on the pure silk habotai of the cascading water. The water is also decorated with sequins and small flowers made from straw veneer, and with mother-of-pearl leaves, rock crystals and silver sequins and stars.

The wooden A-frame support is stretched with painted calico to form a base. Rough blocks of balsa wood represent the rock face of the waterfall, and a piece of driftwood acts as a fallen branch. The silk is gathered together at the top and allowed to flow to the width of the bottom of the support. The rouching at the bottom of the waterfall is created by sewing some of the decorations through the calico backing.

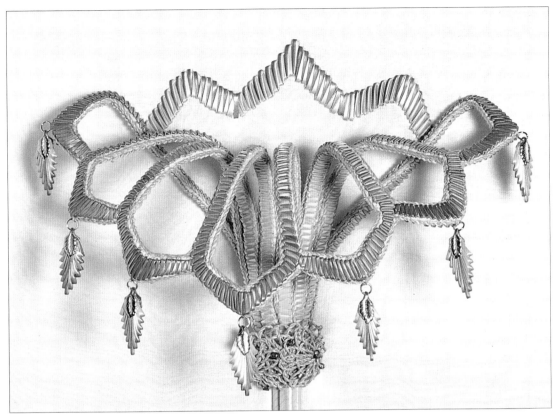

The strength of straw

This design is based on the fan vaults often seen on Gothic architecture. The fan vaults are worked using the porcupine quill technique on two pieces of calico; one piece, the underside, is stitched with natural coloured straw splints, the other with shades of green. The two completed shapes are cut from the calico, leaving a small turn-in (hem) all round. They are sewn together, back to back, with ladder stitch and then straw thread is couched over the seams.

The 'shadow' is also worked in porcupine quill work but is embroidered directly on to the silk background. The pillar consists of three fat straw tubes, each wrapped with straw splints and glued together. The base is a shaped piece of balsa wood covered with straw marquetry – notice how the grain of the straw looks like the natural blemishes of stone blocks. The decoration at the top of the pillar comprises a few overlapping, three-needle roses, decorated with glass beads. Basic spreuers, worked with two shades of green straw, hang from the tips of the fan vault.

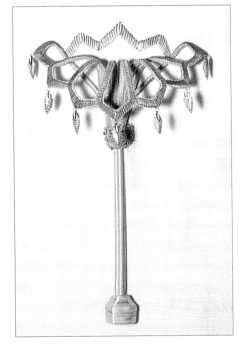

Marquetry

Marquetry is the art of creating pictures and other geometric designs from a range of veneers. These are very thin sheets of wood cut from tree trunks – the colour and grain pattern of each veneer is dependent on the type of tree and the part of the trunk from which it is cut. Pictures are built up by cutting shapes from the veneers and gluing them on a backing board.

Straw marquetry, as we know it, uses veneers made from split and flattened straw stems in the same way as wooden veneers.

Evidence of straw veneer work appears throughout history – examples have been found in ancient Egyptian tombs while others have been dated to Roman times. More recently however, it is known to have flourished in Great Britain two hundred years ago, at the time of the Napoleonic war. Many of the prisoners-of-war were excellent craftsmen, and they spent their weary hours of captivity producing objects of interest which they sold to the local population. Straw was readily available to the prisoners, and they used their skill and ingenuity to create straw marquetry. Today, many of their pieces are still objects of beauty and they are particularly sought after by collectors.

The tools and materials used to produce straw marquetry pictures (see also page 90).

Tools and materials

The essential equipment required for straw marquetry consists of a craft knife and straight edge, an iron, some glue, tracing paper, a pencil and some backing paper or thin card. However, when you want to start making more complex images, you can invest in the other items listed below.

I have shown a few cutters, punches and templates that you can use to create shapes with straw veneers; but there are lots of others that can be employed.

Refer to page 21 for details on how to dye straw.

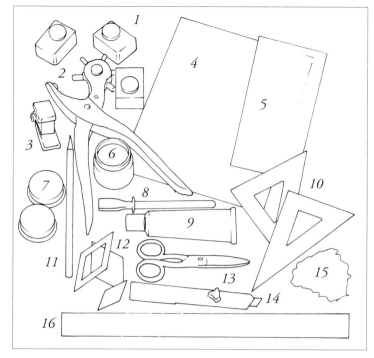

1. Fancy shape punches
2. Leather hole punch
3. Paper punch
4. Graph paper
5. Tracing paper
6. PVA glue
7. Multipurpose dyes
8. Glue spreader
9. General purpose glue
10. Set squares
11. Pencil
12. Metal templates
13. Scissors
14. Craft knife
15. Wire wool
16. Steel ruler
17. Iron (not illustrated)

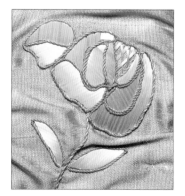

Straw marquetry, such as these two details, can be used as applied decoration on embroideries. However, the initial veneers are glued on scrim instead of paper. The rose (left) is the same design as the embroidery project rose on pages 68–82. Each petal is cut to shape and then couched on with straw threads.

Straw veneer

The veneers used in marquetry are very thin sheets of different coloured wood. However, you can also make veneers from natural and dyed straw and use these in the same way.

In this exercise I show you how to make sheets of veneer, and then how to use them to make a simple design for a card.

Veneers are assembled on to paper or thin card templates and then cut to shape. You will need separate templates for each heart shape in this design.

Pattern used for the heart design. You can make it any size to suit your application. The arrows indicate the direction of the 'grain' of the veneer (the direction of the flattened straw splints).

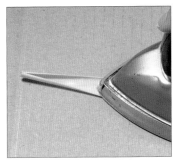

1. Slice lengthwise through the side of damp straws, open them out and flatten them with a hot iron.

2. Use a blunt, flat blade to scrape away the pith from the inside surface of the damp flattened straw strips.

3. Apply PVA glue to the inside surface of the straw strips.

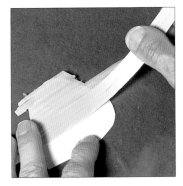

4. Check the grain direction and then stick the straw strips on the *back* of the paper template. Butt adjacent strips as close as possible. When the whole area is covered, leave the veneer under a heavy weight until it is dry.

5. Turn the dry veneer over and cut around the heart shape. Repeat steps 1–5 for the second heart shape using dyed straw.

6. Position the small heart over the large one and use a soft pencil to draw a line round the intersection.

7. Rub the overlapped area of the large heart with wire wool or fine sandpaper to provide a 'key' for the glue.

8. Carefully position and glue the two hearts on to a blank greetings card.

Tip Use coloured paper or card for your templates. Try to tone the colour to that of the straw so that any slight gap between the splints will not notice.

The finished heart card.

Mosaic veneers

Different colours of dyed straw splints (see pages 21) are glued and butted together on graph paper to make a veneer. The veneer is cut across the grain at an angle to create multicoloured strips. These can then be glued together to form a geometric, highly coloured design.

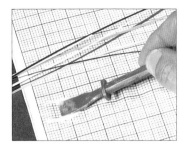

1. Apply a layer of PVA glue to the graph paper, not the straw.

2. Stick splints, side by side, on the graph paper and rub them lightly with a blunt ended tool. Leave under a weight to dry.

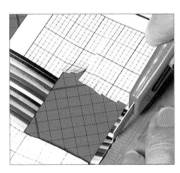

3. Use a craft knife and a straight-edge to cut strips at right angles to the grain. Use the graph paper grid to cut even-width strips.

4. Glue the strips on graph paper. Stagger the strips to make a geometric design.

Tip   Use decorative paper punches and hole punches on sheets of straw veneer to make lots of different shapes. These can be used to adorn a large design (see page 94). You can make straw veneer sequins by gluing veneer to both sides of a sheet of paper.

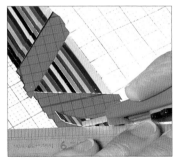

5. Alternatively, cut strips at an angle of 60°. Work from the middle of the veneer and cut two opposing diagonals.

6. Glue the strips on graph paper. Here I have made a chevron pattern by alternating the strips cut from the side of the veneer.

The pattern for this design was developed from a picture of flowers. I made tracings of the outlines of the flower heads and then made straw veneers, using appropriate colours. The small circles were cut with a large hole punch. The brick-like border is a mosaic veneer created by simply alternating strips of red and natural splints.

This proud peacock is a very simple design. It consists of two separate sheets of veneer made by gluing straw strips on muslin. One veneer is cut to the complete outline, the other is just the head and body of the peacock. They are glued to a piece of felt and outlined with straw threads couched with fine sewing thread. Use a large pin to pierce holes through the veneer (from the front to the back) before taking the couching needle and thread through. The decoration consists of small beads, sequins and other small shapes cut from sheets of metallic and mother of pearl plastic. The crown feathers are made from small glass beads threaded on narrow straw splints and wrapped with very fine wire.

This box for playing cards was originally purchased as a plain wooden box. Straw marquetry now covers every surface, transforming it into a beautiful container. The design may appear complicated but, essentially, it is a number of different geometric patterns linked together. The centre design on the lid consists of four triangular veneers made from natural straw splints (see page 91). These are glued together as a rectangle and surrounded by a single splint border. The chevron design is a variation of that shown on page 93.

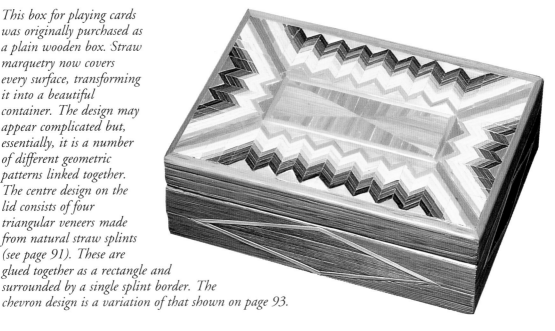

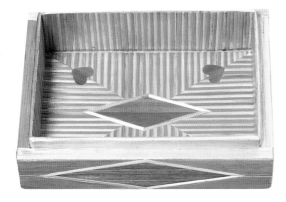

The inside surfaces of the box and its lid are made from sheets of striped veneer which are cut to shape and glued together. The heart shapes are cut with a decorative paper punch.

Index